This book is brought to you by:

hackneyandjones.com

Writers and Publishers of
fiction and non-fiction.

Scan QR Code

Copyright © 2025 by Hackney and Jones. All rights reserved.
No part of this book may be reproduced in any form or by any electronic or mechanical means, including information storage and retrieval systems, without written permission from the authors, except for the use of brief quotations in a book review.

CONTENTS

Introduction		Page 4
Generating Ideas	Character Ideas	Page 25
	Settings	Page 26
	Mind Map	Page 27
	My Complete Plan	Page 28
Setting		Page 29
Themes		Page 30
Emotions		Page 31
Character Traits		Page 32
Main Character		Page 33
Villain		Page 34
Ally		Page 35
Title		Page 36
Colours		Page 37
Numbers		Page 38
Shapes		Page 39
Days Of The Week		Page 40

CONTENTS

Repetition/Rule Of Three	**Page 41**
Character Goal	**Page 42**
Obstacle Ideas For Each Step	**Page 43**
Main Character (Goals/Obstacles/Consequences)	**Page 44**
The Inciting Event	**Page 45**
Endings	**Page 46**
S.A.T.P.I.N. Ideas	**Page 47**
Phonics Ideas	**Page 48**
Similes	**Page 49**
Syllables	**Page 50**
Patterned Language	**Page 51**
Rhyme	**Page 52**
Alliteration	**Page 53**
Onomatopoeia	**Page 54**
Your Story Outline	**Page 55**
Write Your Story	**Page 59**
Example Story	**Page 66**

INTRODUCTION

EMBARK ON YOUR ADVENTURE!

INTRODUCTION

WHY ARE YOU HERE?

We are assuming you are here because you want to write amazing children's stories, right?

Maybe you have tried lots of things before or maybe this is your introduction to children's story writing.

Either way, welcome!

THE AIM OF THIS WORKBOOK:

This workbook aims to take you from a blank page to a fully written children's story outline, step by step, and for you to enjoy it along the way.

It is a streamlined roadmap to creating an awesome children's story from scratch – with never seen before techniques. We know this because we invented them!

Sound good?

THIS WORKBOOK IS MADE UP OF THREE PARTS:

1- **The Introduction** – so you know what you're doing and why.

2 - **The Planning** - what elements of Early Years language to include.

3 - **The Outline** – how to structure your children's story.

INTRODUCTION

WHY WE ARE DIFFERENT:

We have read books about creative writing, taken courses etc. but found them far too 'fluffy'.

We wanted actionable steps. *Can you relate?*

So this workbook GIVES YOU the actual content and ideas so that you have inspiration at every step, rather than leaving you to come up with things yourself - ensuring zero writer's block!

THESE ARE THE VITAL ELEMENTS FOR YOUR CHILDREN'S STORY:

- **Characters** - Are they interesting? Will your readers enjoy reading about them?

- **Settings** - Where does your story take place? In the city? Space? In the country?

- **Plot** - The sequence of events in your story to drive it forward.

- **Goal** - What does your main character want/need to achieve and why?

- **Conflict** - What/who stands in your main character's way of getting what they want?

- **Consequences** - What happens if your main character doesn't get what they want?

INTRODUCTION

IF YOU ONLY REMEMBER THREE THINGS BY THE END OF THIS PROCESS:

- Your reader comes first – always. Make sure you create a children's story that keeps your young readers guessing, but one that's not too complicated. They (and the parents/carers) are investing time, energy and sometimes money reading your work. Don't worry – we've got you covered with **EVERYTHING!** Just follow the steps.

- Follow the roadmap we give you, but don't be afraid to create your own tracks as well. We personally advise outlining your stories - it really helps with writer's block - but when you are confident with the plot/scenes etc. don't be afraid to follow your inspiration.

OUR MOTTO FOR AVOIDING WRITER'S BLOCK:

IF YOU CAN...

Use your imagination: Think of an awesome character from your imagination.

IF YOU CAN'T...

Use your observation: Think of a character you have read in a book or seen in the movies.

IF YOU NEED...

Resources: Use the resources on each planning page to help you with ideas.

WHO ARE WE?

Hi, I'm **Claire Hackney** and I am a former teacher turned full-time novelist and publisher from Cheshire, England. My background in teaching English, Drama, and Media Studies fuels my storytelling passion.

My intrigue for history finds a home in my work, particularly in our 1950s-inspired novels (Meet Me at 10 etc.). Beyond this, I'm set to embark on an exciting path, including finishing the upcoming DI Rachel Morrison crime thriller series. My first children's book, 'Katie and the Kite,' was released in 2024.

Find me at:

TWITTER: @ClaireHac
INSTAGRAM: @clairehackneyauthor
WEBSITE: hackneyandjones.com

Hi, I'm **Vicky Jones** and I'm from Essex, England. I joined the Royal Navy at 20 but felt something was missing. So, I decided to make a bold list of 300 things to do, and my life transformed, especially after attending a writing group to help me write a novel which went on to become a bestseller.

I have also written songs for iTunes and YouTube. One of my songs, "House of Cards," is centred around the theme of bullying. I also co-wrote 'Meet Me at 10' with Claire, a book which deals with controversial societal issues.

I love to travel and have been to around 50 countries - so far! I have also also gained a psychology and criminology degree from The Open University.

Although now living in Cheshire, I keep ties with my Essex roots.

My journey is all about being creative, brave, and discovering myself.

My first children's book, 'Katie and the Kite,' was released in 2024.

Find me at:

TWITTER: @VickyJones7
INSTAGRAM: @vickytjones
WEBSITE: hackneyandjones.com

OUR WRITING JOURNEY

WE HAVE WRITTEN FICTION AND NON-FICTION BOOKS!

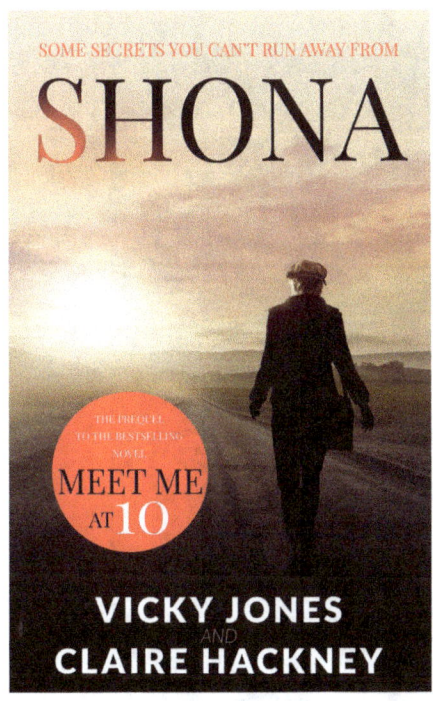
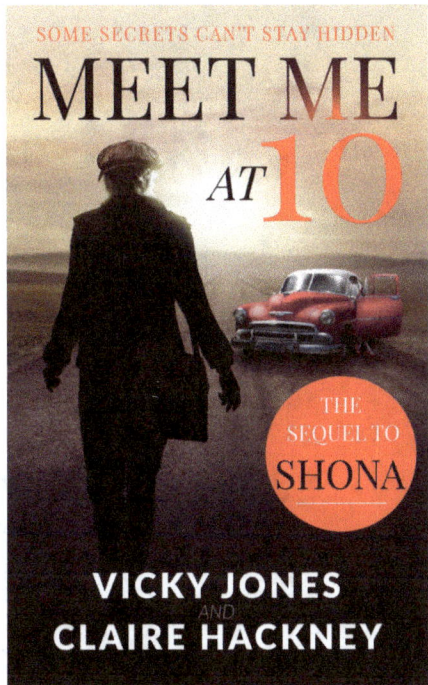
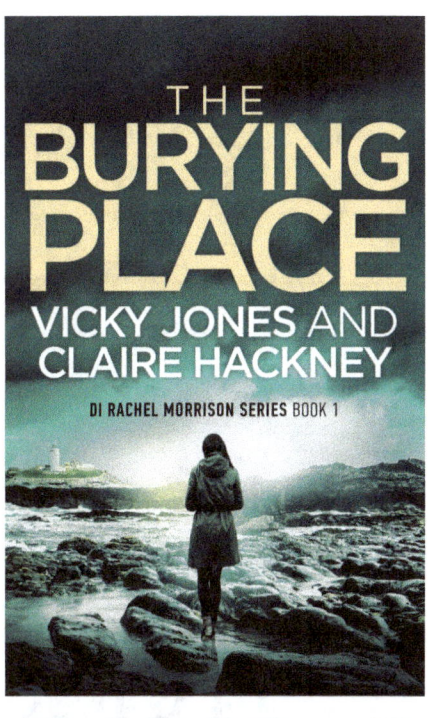

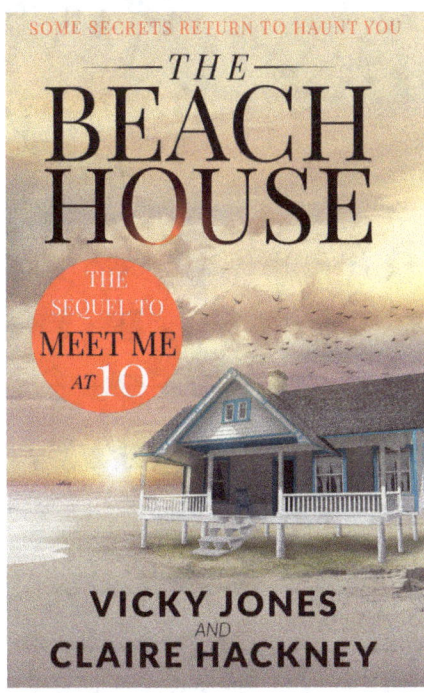
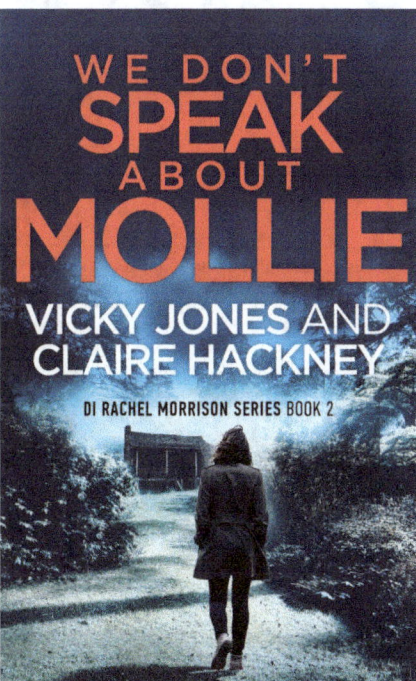

OUR EXPERIENCE IN WRITING CHILDREN'S STORIES

WE HAVE ALSO WRITTEN OUR OWN SERIES OF EARLY YEARS CHILDREN'S BOOKS

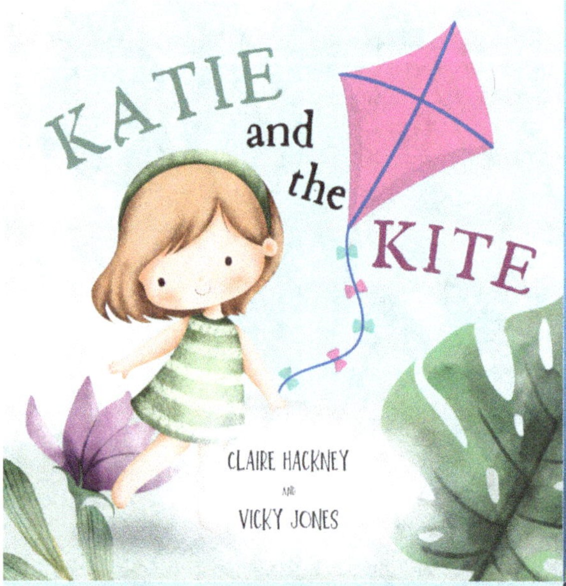

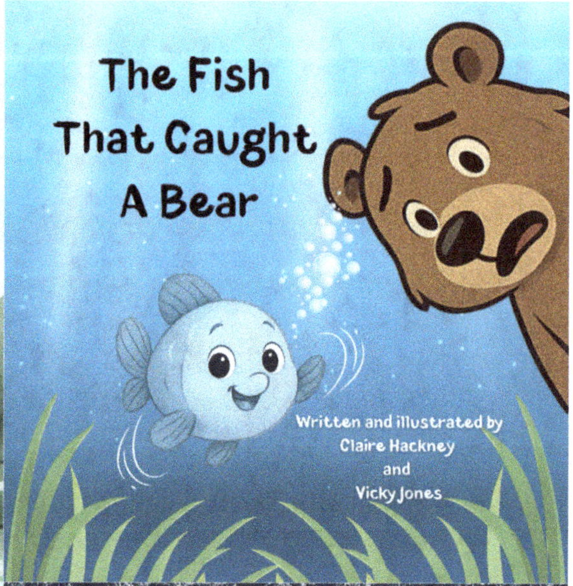

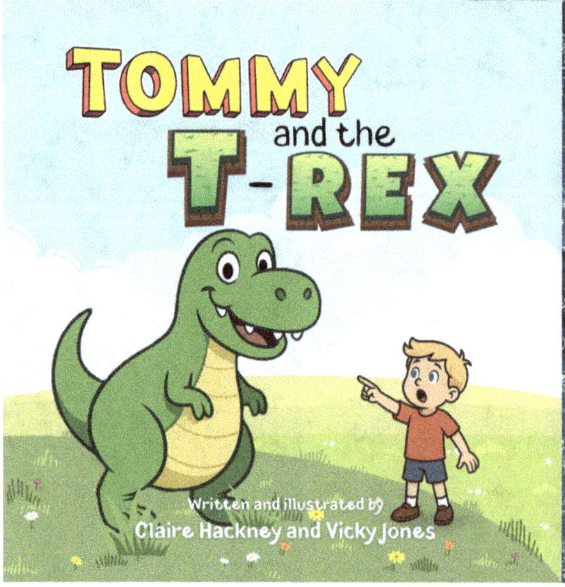

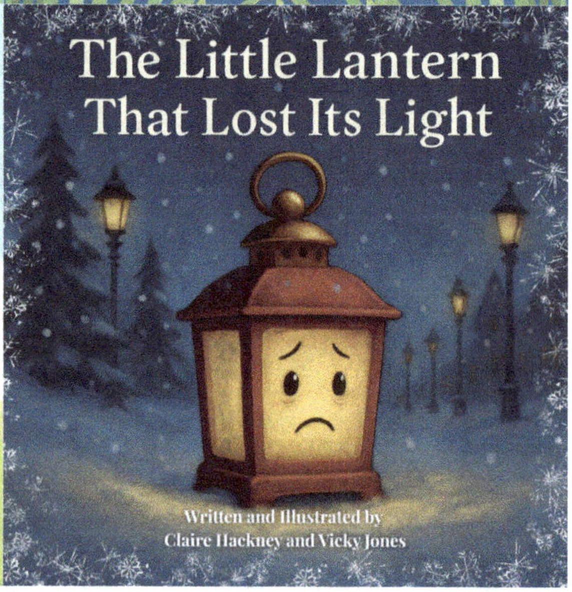

HOW TO BE A GREAT CHILDREN'S AUTHOR

To be a good storyteller you need to get in touch with your inner child.

THIS IS VERY IMPORTANT.

You need to try to see the world through the eyes of a child.

If you 'think' like an adult, and 'write like an adult,' your story will be only appropriate for adults.

MYTH BUSTING

MYTH	TRUTH
Writing children's stories is easy.	Crafting impactful children's stories takes practice. Writing concisely while conveying emotions and themes can be challenging.
I need to be an excellent writer.	You don't need qualifications to be a writer. You don't need to have 'done well at school.' If you're worried about spelling, grammar etc. software etc. can help with that.
Only published authors are "real" writers.	If you write, you're a writer. Publication isn't the only measure of success.
Writing children's stories has no impact.	Children's stories can evoke emotions, explore themes, and leave lasting impressions.
Picture books are so easy to write!	Picture books may seem simple to write, but there is a complexity, a structure, and a formula for a good story to make it good enough for a child to enjoy.
Writing children's stories is not "serious" writing.	Children's stories are respected literature. They pack a punch.
You need a degree in writing to be good at it.	Passion and willingness to learn matter more.
You must be original in every aspect.	Uniqueness comes from your perspective and voice.

Remember: Writing is a journey. Embrace your love for writing, be persistent, and trust in your ability to create meaningful stories.

THE BENEFITS OF CHILDREN'S STORIES AND PICTURE BOOKS

- They can bring families together and help children's vocabulary.

- It can create a bond at bedtime for parents/carers and their child.

- They can help soothe children to sleep.

- It can be picture book stories that introduce children to language and sounds.

- They can spark a child's imagination.

Globally, picture books outsell adult titles.

Children are CRAVING stories!

The industry isn't saturated by any means.

Picture books are the oldest form of storytelling. Think of cave paintings.

They are picture books on a wall.

THE BENEFITS OF CHILDREN'S STORIES AND PICTURE BOOKS

Picture books are a child's introduction to language and art. They can help them start learning about sounds, numbers, shapes, and emotions etc.

Picture books can help children cope with emotion and challenging events in their lives, such as the death of a parent or grandparent.

Even using (appropriate) humour can help with complex feelings.

Be careful though. AVOID using innuendo. You want both adults and children to be laughing at the same thing.

The whole story doesn't have to be funny, it can be sad at times. But children or animals being naughty will always go down well in stories.

Some picture books are text-heavy, and some are picture-heavy.

Some invite parents and children to answer questions and have a discussion about certain topics or themes.

Stories can be both educational and entertaining.

FAMOUS CHILDREN'S STORIES AND WHY THEY ARE POPULAR

"The Gruffalo" by Julia Donaldson:

'The Gruffalo' tells the story of a clever mouse who outwits various predators by inventing a fearsome creature called the Gruffalo. It is loved for its humourous rhymes, engaging plot, and memorable characters.

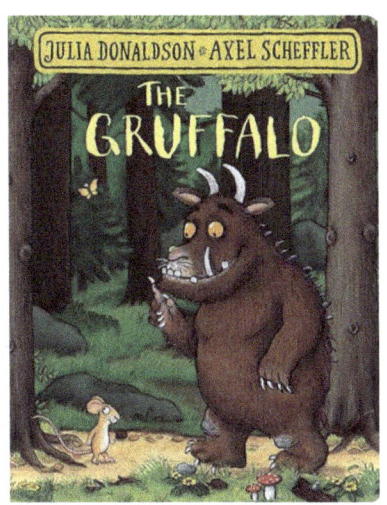

"The Tale of Peter Rabbit" by Beatrix Potter:

This story follows the mischievous adventures of Peter Rabbit as he sneaks into Mr. McGregor's garden against his mother's warnings. Its charming illustrations and timeless tale of curiosity and consequence have captivated readers for generations.

"The Very Hungry Caterpillar" by Eric Carle

This story follows the journey of a caterpillar as it eats its way through various foods before transforming into a butterfly. It is loved for its colourful collage-style illustrations and simple, repetitive text.

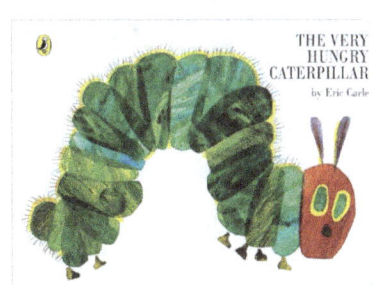

WHERE COULD WRITING CHILDREN'S STORIES TAKE YOU?

- **Publication:** Your children's story could be published by traditional or self-publishing routes, reaching young readers worldwide.

- **Recognition and awards:** Exceptional stories may win awards, boosting your credibility and opening doors to more opportunities.

- **Adaptation:** Successful stories may be adapted into movies, TV shows, or other media, expanding your story's reach and impact.

- **Educational use:** Your story might be used in schools and educational programmes to promote literacy and learning.

- **Speaking engagements:** You could be invited to speak at schools and events, inspiring young readers and fellow writers.

- **Workshops and teaching:** Share your expertise by leading workshops on children's storytelling.

- **Merchandising:** Popular characters could lead to merchandise opportunities, generating additional income.

- **Translations and global reach:** Your story might be translated into multiple languages, reaching a diverse audience worldwide.

- **Impact on young minds:** Shape young minds with your stories, instilling values and fostering a love for reading.

- **Personal fulfilment:** Ultimately, writing children's stories can bring personal satisfaction, knowing you've entertained and inspired young readers.

WHAT HAS STOPPED YOU BEFORE?

There is a reason why you are here. Something has stopped you from either starting your story or writing 'The End,' right?

It is useful to know what those reasons are so you can progress.

Here are the most common reasons writers struggle. We will help you solve them all:

- **Self-doubt:**

  - **Issue:** Many new writers grapple with self-doubt, questioning their abilities and fearing that their writing won't meet their own or others' expectations.
  - **Impact:** This can lead to hesitation, perfectionism, and a reluctance to begin or complete a story.

- **Overwhelm:**

  - **Issue:** The sheer scope of writing a story, with its characters, plot, and settings, can be overwhelming for new writers.
  - **Impact:** Feeling overwhelmed can result in procrastination and a sense of being unable to navigate the complexities of storytelling.

- **Lack of structure or planning:**

  - **Issue:** Some new writers may dive into writing without a clear plan or structure, leading to uncertainty and difficulty in maintaining a coherent narrative.
  - **Impact:** Without a roadmap, writers may get lost or discouraged during the writing process.

- **Fear of failure or criticism:**

  - **Issue:** The fear of failure or criticism can be paralysing for new writers. The thought of negative feedback or rejection can hinder creative expression.
  - **Impact:** Writers may be hesitant to take risks, experiment with their writing, or submit their work for fear of judgment.

WHAT HAS STOPPED YOU BEFORE?

- **Time management challenges:**

  - **Issue:** Balancing writing with other responsibilities, such as work or studies, can be challenging for new writers.
  - **Impact:** Limited time may result in sporadic writing habits, making it difficult to maintain momentum and complete a story.

- **The blank page:**

  - **Issue:** Confronting a blank page can be intimidating, and the pressure to start with the perfect sentence can be paralysing.
  - **Impact:** The blank page challenge can stifle creativity and prevent writers from taking the initial steps in their storytelling journey.

- **Confidence:**

  - **Issue:** A lack of confidence in one's writing abilities can hinder the creative process, making it difficult to express ideas with conviction.
  - **Impact:** Low confidence may lead to second-guessing, self-censorship, and reluctance to share one's writing with others. Building confidence is crucial for a writer's growth.

Put simply... This workbook will help you in the following ways:

- You won't write a whole story, you will write a scene, then another and then another.

- You will join them together and they just happen to create an engaging story!

- We take all the stress and overwhelm out of the process, so relax and enjoy!

THINGS TO <u>AVOID</u>

- Waffling - Every word must count, as you have to "get to the good bit" quicker than in longer-form stories.

- The word count for children's picture books tends to be an average of around 100-600 words; sometimes more, sometimes less. There are some at around 1000 words.

- Sexism, classism, racism, dangerous situations that kids may copy, scary scenes, horror, gore, drugs, sex, rude words, and offensive words **must be avoided** in your story.

All pretty basic, right?

WHAT THE BESTSELLERS DO

If a book is a bestseller, it means it is popular, right?

If it is popular on Amazon then more than a few people like it, would that be fair to say?

If we study the similarities between the top 5 bestsellers, we will *AUTOMATICALLY* know what readers want.

Always remember…

Your reader comes first. Why?

If your book/story isn't what they want, they won't buy it, or like it, and may leave a 1-star review on Amazon.

Emulate the best but **DO NOT COPY** them - this is important!

You want inspiration and information.

THE PURPOSE

If we know the similarities between popular picture books, with regards to storylines, front cover, characters, number of pages, types of illustrations etc., then we are on the right path to success.

We know if we included even a couple of those elements, our story could be a winner!

The bestsellers are giving you a treasure map to success.

There's no need to 'see' if something works, we have the answers right in front of us.

WHAT THE BESTSELLERS DO

Go to Amazon.

Type in the search bar: childrens picture books ages 3-5 years

Look at what comes up.

You want to avoid the 'sponsored' results - they are ads and are not there organically.

These are some of the results...

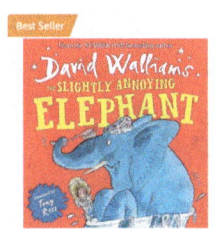
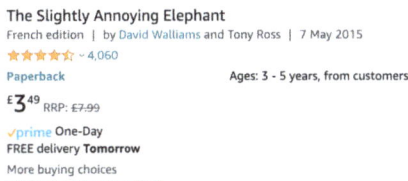

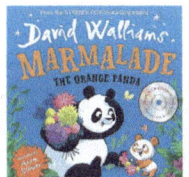

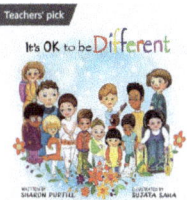

Let's see if they have anything in common at all and list these elements...

WHAT THE BESTSELLERS DO

Front covers: Colourful/bright.

Main characters: Animals on the cover (apart from one).

Titles: Ask questions 'The Koala Who Could' (Do what?), 'The Slightly Annoying Elephant' (why annoying?), 'Marmalade the Orange Panda' (Why orange?)

Themes: Difference, courage, adventure.

Font: Nice and big, easy to read, child-friendly font.

Being aware of the following will make your story popular with readers.

Front covers: Colourful/bright. I will design my cover to include ....
....

Main characters: Animals on the cover. I will include ....
on my front cover.

Titles: Ask questions. My story title could ask the question ....
....

Themes: Difference, courage, adventure. My theme could include ....
....

Font: Nice and big, easy to read, child-friendly font. I will use the font ....
in my story.

Just by filling in the above, your story will be so much better than other beginners as they will not have used this method.

You are meeting the demand of your target market and giving them stories they are actively looking for.

This equals SUCCESS!

Planning Your Story

4 steps to an epic story idea!

The secret formula:

- **What if?** (Character + Goal)

- **And then?** (Curiosity/Discovery)

- **But...** (Peril + Danger + Villain?)

- **However...** (Plot twist)

GENERATING IDEAS

Character Ideas

Train	Bear	Car	Turtle
Fireman	Bunny	Unicorn	Frog
Mermaid	Cat	Witch	Duck
Shark	Dog	Knight	Penguin
Pirate	Mouse	Horse	Tiger
Princess	Fairy	Owl	Giraffe
Dragon	Wizard	Fox	Ladybug
Dinosaur	Robot	Wolf	Superhero

 **Now lock in your idea**

Character: ....

What if? ....

And then? ....

But: ....

However: ....

GENERATING IDEAS

Settings

Underwater	City	Sky	Rainforest	Bakery
Forest	Village	Desert	Pirate ship	Market
Farm	Park	Island	Spaceship	Treehouse
Jungle	Zoo	Cave	Train station	Haunted house
Castle	Circus	River	Fire station	Dragon's lair
Space	School	Lake	Hospital	Magic shop
Beach	House	Swamp	Library	Treasure island
Mountain	Garden	Snowy land	Playground	Toy store

 **Now lock in your idea**

Setting: ....

What if? ....

And then? ....

But: ....

However: ....

GENERATING IDEAS

Mind Map

Boy	Puppy
Girl	Mermaid
Fairy	Astronaut
Cub	Pirate

Place one of the words from the table (or one of your own) in the middle of the mind map and then write as many things you can think of that are associated with that word.

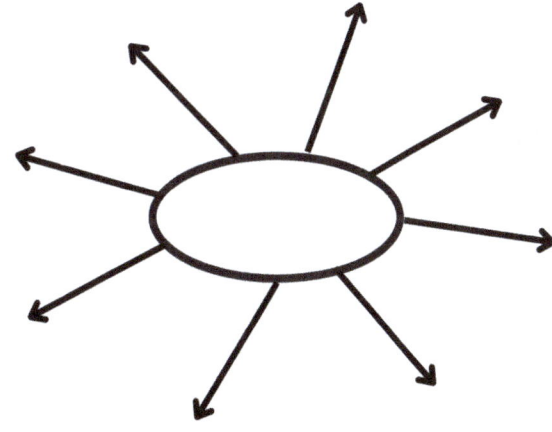

 **Now lock in your idea**

What if? ....

And then? ....

But: ....

However: ....

GENERATING IDEAS

My Complete Idea

What if? The main character needs to do something (goal).

And then? The story progresses towards the goal/mission - sparks curiosity.

But: Something 'bad' happens.

However: All is not what it seems (the villain could actually be nice, etc.) - the plot twist!

 ## Now lock in your idea

What if? ....

And then? ....

But: ....

However: ....

This is my favourite idea because: ....

Some ideas I think I may want to include in this story: (Names, endings, scenes etc.)

....
....
....
....

28

SETTINGS

Underwater	City	Sky	Rainforest	Bakery
Forest	Village	Desert	Pirate ship	Market
Farm	Park	Island	Spaceship	Treehouse
Jungle	Zoo	Cave	Train station	Haunted house
Castle	Circus	River	Fire station	Dragon's lair
Space	School	Lake	Hospital	Magic shop
Beach	House	Swamp	Library	Treasure island
Mountain	Garden	Snowy land	Playground	Toy store

 **Now lock in your idea**

The main setting of my story is: ....

What are the main colours in my setting? ....

How could I describe this setting? ....

Other settings I may include: ....

29

THEMES

Friendship	Growing up	Being yourself	Fairness
Sharing	Teamwork	Problem-solving	Patience
Courage	Love	Caring for animals	Gratitude
Kindness	Honesty	Exploring nature	Creativity
Family	Bravery	Happiness	Belonging
Adventure	Curiosity	Overcoming fears	Discovery
Imagination	Acceptance	Respect	Forgiveness
Helping others	Trying new things	Responsibility	Joy

Then pick the **opposite** theme to your main theme:

- Friendship - Loneliness
- Courage - Fear
- Kindness - Cruelty
- Adventure - Boredom
- Imagination - Dullness
- Family - Isolation
- Sharing - Selfishness
- Discovery - Ignorance
- Honesty - Deceit
- Acceptance - Rejection

 # Now lock in your idea

My theme idea is: ....

....

How can I show this? (Success at the end) ....

....

The opposite of this theme is: ....

....

How can I show this? (In the beginning) ....

....

EMOTIONS

Happiness	Surprise	Curiosity	Nervousness
Sadness	Worry	Jealousy	Relief
Anger	Joy	Hope	Boredom
Fear	Loneliness	Silliness	Cheerfulness
Excitement	Bravery	Grumpiness	Guilt
Love	Confusion	Confidence	Trust
Shyness	Frustration	Disappointment	Excitement
Pride	Calmness	Kindness	Kind
Peace	Embarrassment	Eagerness	Annoyance
Wonder	Tiredness	Playfulness	Sympathy
Doubt	Upset	Determination	Contentment

Now lock in your idea

Pick the main emotion you want to show in your story: ....
....
....
....

How can we 'show' evidence of this emotion in your story (scene ideas): ....
....
....
....

CHARACTER TRAITS

Funny	Silly	Bossy	Slow	Calm	Bold
Clumsy	Loud	Gentle	Clever	Wild	Caring
Brave	Quiet	Sneaky	Forgetful	Polite	Greedy
Shy	Curious	Cheerful	Helpful	Noisy	Patient
Smart	Lazy	Messy	Playful	Friendly	Chatty
Kind	Happy	Neat	Serious	Stubborn	Imaginative
Grumpy	Sad	Fast	Bouncy	Timid	Creative

GOALS

Find way home	Rescue someone	Learn to fly	Share a toy
Save the world	Win a race	Build something	Climb a mountain
Make a friend	Fix a mess	Stop a storm	Cross a river
Find a treasure	Catch a thief	Get to school	Bake a cake
Solve a mystery	Sing a song	Escape a trap	Wake a friend

SKILLS

Can fly	Climbs anything	Changes colours	Glows bright
Talks to pets	Bounces high	Jumps really far	Grows big
Runs super fast	Sees in the dark	Hears tiny sounds	Draws things alive
Turns invisible	Swims like a fish	Makes rainbows	Freezes stuff
Sings magic songs	Builds machines	Shrinks small	Fixes anything

MAIN CHARACTER

 ## Now lock in your idea

My main character is a: ....

Character name: ....

Main character NEEDS to (goal): ....

Because: ....

Consequences if they don't achieve goal? ....

Who/what is standing in their way? ....

What will they need to do to/have to overcome this (theme?): ....
....

2 words to describe your main character:

1: ....

How can you 'show' this characteristic in a scene? ....

2: ....

How can you 'show' this characteristic in a scene? ....

What does your character **LOVE** and why? ....

What does your character **HATE** and why? ....

What skills do they have? ....

How will my character act at the **beginning** of the story (opposite of main theme) - what could they be doing? ....
....

How will they act at the **end?** (Main theme) - What could they be doing? ....
....

VILLAIN

 ## Now lock in your idea

My villain is a: ....

Villain's name: ....

Villain NEEDS to (goal): ....

Because: ....

Consequences if they don't achieve goal? ....

Who/what is standing in their way? ....

What will they need to do to/have to overcome this (theme?): ....
....
....

2 words to describe your villain:

1: ....

How can you 'show' this characteristic in a scene? ....

2: ....

How can you 'show' this characteristic in a scene? ....

What does your villain **LOVE** and why? ....

What does your villain **HATE** and why? ....

What skills do they have? ....

How will my villain act at the **beginning** of the story (opposite of main theme) - what could they be doing? ....
....

How will they act at the **end**? (Main theme) - What could they be doing? ....
....

ALLY

 **Now lock in your idea**

The ally in my story is a: ....

Ally's name: ....

They help the main character by (wisdom, powers): ....
....
....
....
....
....
....

Scene ideas to show the ally helping main character in this story (Think of the main character's worst fear coming true): ....
....
....
....
....
....
....

TITLE

Here are some formulas to help you if you haven't thought of your own:

Formula 1

[Character's Name or Descriptor] + [Action or Problem] + [Setting or Context]

eg: "Sammy the Super Snail Saves the Garden"

Formula 2

[Adjective] + [Noun] + [Adventure or Journey]

"Curious Cat's Adventure in Space"

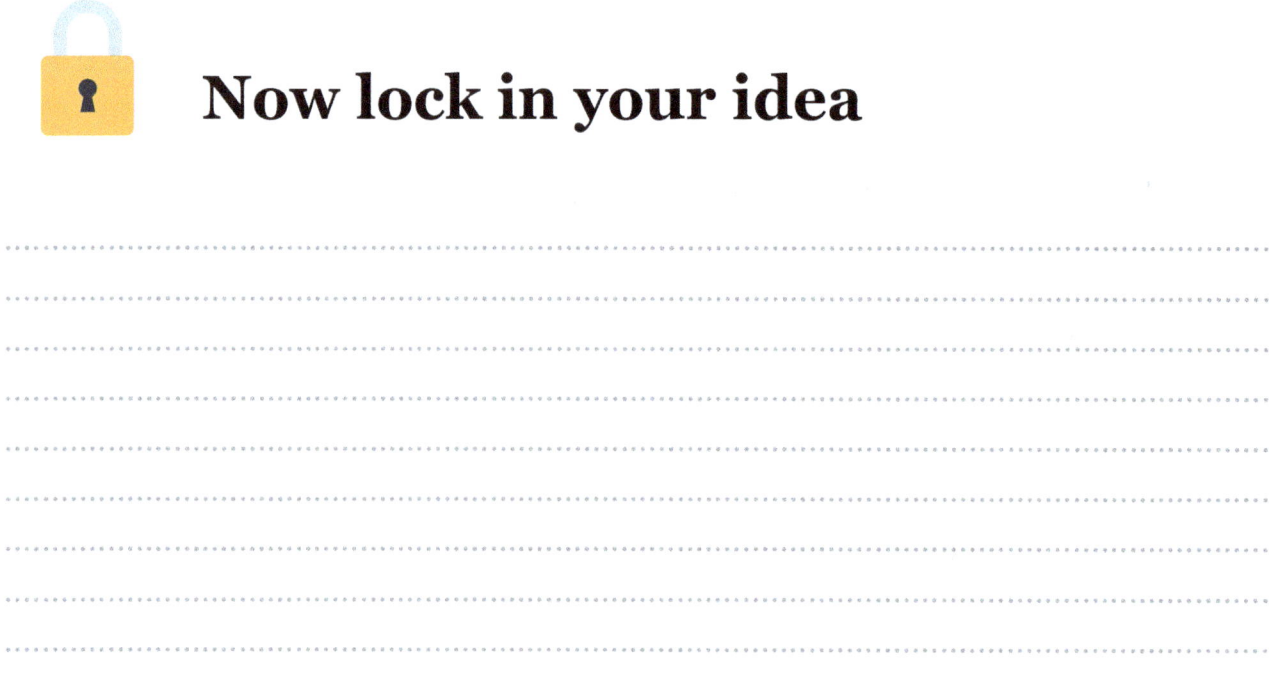 **Now lock in your idea**

....
....
....
....
....
....
....
....

COLOURS

- **Red:** Apple, Fire engine, Tomato, Ladybug.

- **Orange:** Orange (fruit), Pumpkin, Carrot, Goldfish.

- **Yellow:** Sun, Banana, Lemon, Duck.

- **Green:** Grass, Frog, Leaf, Lime.

- **Blue:** Sky, Water, Blueberry, Whale.

- **Indigo (Dark blue-purple):** Night sky, Grapes, Jacket, Crayon.

- **Violet (Purple):** Plum, Balloon, Flower, Butterfly.

Examples:

"The shiny red apple tastes good."

"The juicy orange fruit is sweet."

"The soft green grass feels nice."

"The big blue sky looks pretty."

"The pretty purple flower smells good."

Now lock in your idea

What are some of the main colours in your story/setting?

....
....
....

How could you describe some of the main objects: **"Bright yellow circle sun…"**

....
....
....

NUMBERS

- **Counting friends:** Characters count how many pals join the adventure (e.g., "Tiko meets 3 buddies").

- **Ticking clock:** Counting down to danger (e.g., "3 seconds before the splash!").

- **Animal parade:** Number of animals marching by (e.g., "7 ducks waddle past").

- **Door number:** Add numbered doors to choose (e.g., "Door 2 opens wide" or "3 doors to pick").

- **Number of sounds:** Count noises they hear or make (e.g., "6 loud bangs" or "3 soft hoots").

- **Number of places:** List spots they go (e.g., "2 caves to explore" or "3 hills to climb").

- **Countdown:** "3,2,1... GO!"

- **Number of colours:** Highlight colours with numbers (e.g., "5 red leaves" or "2 blue fish").

🔒 Now lock in your idea

Some ideas of where I can use numbers in my story:

....
....
....
....
....

SHAPES

- **Circle:** Seen in suns, moons, wheels, and faces; easy to spot and name.
    - Eg: *"The bright circle sun wakes everybody up."*

- **Square:** Found in windows, blocks, and boxes; a basic, everyday shape.
    - Eg: *"The square window lets light in."*

- **Triangle:** Common in trees, roofs, and hats; pointy and fun to point out.
    - Eg: *"The triangle-shaped tree stands tall."*

- **Rectangle:** Appears in doors, books, and beds; familiar.
    - Eg: *"The rectangle-shaped door swings open."*

- **Star:** Known from stars, stickers, and sparkles.
    - Eg: *"The stars sparkle high in the sky."*

Now lock in your idea

Which shapes are common in your story setting? Eg: circle, square, etc.
....
....
....
....

Which objects display these shapes? Eg: the sun, moon, etc.
....
....
....
....

DAYS OF THE WEEK

- **Daily activities:**

  - Tie each day to something the character does. *"On Sundays, Katie loves to go to the park."*

- **Time passing:**

  - Show days counting up or down to an event. *"Today is Tuesday, only 4 days until the party!"*

- **Weather changes:**

  - Match days to what's outside. *"It was a wet and windy Wednesday."*

- **Visitors or friends:**

  - Have different pals show up on each day. *"Katie loved visiting Mary on Saturdays."*

🔒 Now lock in your idea

What ideas could you have to include one or more days of the week?

....
....
....
....
....
....

REPETITION/RULE OF THREE

Ideas:

- **Repetition:**

"*Boing! Boing! Boing!*" after each jump.

"*Bunny hops, hops, hops every day!*"

"*Splash! Splash! Splash! goes the puddle.*"

- **Rule of 3:**

"*Bunny jumps once—too short. Twice—too low. Three times—over the puddle!*"

"*Boom, crash, splash—here comes the rain!*"

"*Tiko sees a small hill, a medium hill, a big hill—he climbs them all!*"

🔒 Now lock in your idea

Ideas for repetition:
....
....
....
....

Ideas for the rule of 3:
....
....
....
....

CHARACTER GOAL

Start with your goal.

My main character needs to: (Goal) ....
....
....

What does the 'ending' look like if they achieve this goal? ....
....
....

What are the 3 logical **steps** my main character has to do/take in order to achieve the goal?

1: ....

2: ....

3: ....

These are some scenes for your story. They will ensure it will flow.

Notes/ideas to include:

....
....
....
....

OBSTACLE IDEAS FOR EACH STEP

- **Lost item:** Something they need (like a shoe or a map) goes missing.

- **Shy moment:** They feel too nervous to ask for help or start.

- **Small mess:** A spill or clutter blocks their first move (e.g., toys on the floor).

- **Noisy distraction:** A loud pet or sibling interrupts their focus.

- **Tricky path:** A puddle, wobbly bridge, or sticky mud slows them down.

- **Missing tool:** They realise they don't have what they need (e.g., no spoon for mixing).

- **Grumpy helper:** A friend or animal refuses to cooperate at first.

- **Little scare:** A shadow or strange sound makes them pause.

- **Big block:** A closed gate, tall step, or locked box stands in the way.

- **Time crunch:** The sun's setting or a grown-up calls them to hurry.

- **Last doubt:** They wonder if they can really finish (e.g., "It's too hard!").

- **Weather twist:** Rain, wind, or a sudden chill threatens their success.

- **Heavy object:** Something they need to move (like a big rock or a full basket) is too heavy.

- **Sneaky hider:** A playful friend or pet keeps hiding what they're looking for.

- **Broken thing:** A tool or toy they need (like a crayon or wheel) breaks.

- **Too dark:** A shadowy spot or lights going out makes it hard to see.

- **Slippery spot:** A wet floor or icy patch makes them slip or hesitate.

- **Wrong turn:** They pick the wrong path or door and have to backtrack.

- **Tangled mess:** Strings, vines, or a messy blanket get them stuck.

- **Loud noise:** A sudden bang or crash startles them into stopping.

- **Too quiet:** Everything's so silent that they feel unsure about moving forward.

- **Funny mix-up:** They grab the wrong thing (e.g., a sock instead of a hat) by mistake.

MAIN CHARACTER

GOALS, OBSTACLES AND CONSEQUENCES

 ## Now lock in your idea

Start with your goal: ....

My main character needs to: (Goal) ....

What does the 'ending' look like if they achieve this goal? ....
....
....

What are the **3 logical steps** my main character has to do/take in order to achieve the goal?

Step 1: ....

Obstacle: ....

Consequence: ....

Step 2: ....

Obstacle: ....

Consequence: ....

Step 3: ....

Obstacle: ....

Consequence (Ending): ....

THE INCITING EVENT

The inciting event is the event that disrupts the main character's ordinary world and sets the story's main conflict in motion, forcing them to act and begin their journey.

It is a pivotal turning point that irrevocably changes the main character's life, making it impossible to return to their previous status quo.

For example: The family pet goes missing, a mysterious letter arrives in the post, or a favourite toy suddenly starts talking.

My character's goal is: ....

What are some inciting event ideas?

1: ....

2: ....

3: ....

Pick your favourite: Idea number: ....

🔒 Now lock in your idea

My inciting event in a bit more detail is: ....
....
....
....
....
....

This is also your beginning sorted!

ENDINGS

You may have an idea for your ending, but have a look at these and think if you want to stick with it or change it.

- **Happy ending:** Characters achieve their goals and find joy.

- **Unexpected twist**: A surprise revelation changes everything.

- **Open-ended conclusion:** Leaves room for imagination.

- **Lesson learned:** Characters reflect and grow.

- **Bittersweet ending:** Mixed emotions but resolution.

- **Return to normalcy:** Characters back home, changed.

- **Circle of friendship:** Unity and acceptance celebrated.

- **Heroic triumph:** Protagonist overcomes fear and wins.

- **Magical transformation:** Ends with wonder and possibility.

- **Resolution through friendship:** Characters bond, solving problems together.

 ## Now lock in your idea

What happens exactly? Could it be the opposite of what the reader's expect?

My (new) ending is: ....
....
....

What (if anything) do I have to change/alter BEFOREHAND to make this ending realistic? ....
....
....

S.A.T.P.I.N. IDEAS

S.A.T.P.I.N. refers to the first six letters and sounds that are taught to children when they begin learning to read through phonics: s, a, t, p, i, and n.

This sequence is used because these letters are common and allow children to start blending and segmenting sounds to create many simple words

S	A	T	P	I	N
Sun	Apple	Top	Pig	In	Nap
See	Ant	Tap	Pat	It	No
Sit	All	Tall	Pan	Ice	Nut
Sad	At	Ten	Pet	Is	Nose
Sip	And	Tip	Pin	If	Net
Sand	Ask	Tin	Pop	Ill	Nod
Sing	Ate	Tag	Pip	Ink	Nip
Sock	Arm	Toe	Pen	Icy	Nail
Soft	Air	Tug	Pup	Into	Neck
Seed	Aim	Tail	Pad	Iron	Need
Sail	Art	Take	Pay	Idea	Nice
Sea	Ash	Talk	Pea	Idol	Nine

🔒 Now lock in your idea

Scene ideas for my story including S.A.T.P.I.N. words:

1: ....

2: ....

3: ....

PHONICS IDEAS

Vowel Pattern	Word Examples
Short 'a'	Fan, Pan, Man, Cat, Rat, Bat, Hat, Mat, Mad, Bad, Tag, Dad, Can, Man
Short 'e'	Pen, Ten, When, Bet, Let, Jet, Bed, Ted, Men, Get, Met, Wed, Red, Hen
Short 'i'	Bit, Pit, Fit, Fin, Win, Pin, Lit, Jig, Hit, Mix, Big, Dig, Pill, Mit, Wit, Din
Short 'o'	Pot, Lot, Dot, Hop, Shop, Drop, Top, Box, Hog, Frog, Tog, Pop, Mop, Cop
Short 'u'	Fun, Run, Sun, Bun, Up, Cup, Bug, Rug, Hug, Mug, Cut, Nut, Hut, Gum
Long 'a'	Fail, Rain, Pail, Tale, Whale, Make, Cake, Lake, Take, Make, Rake, Name
Long 'e'	Feet, Sheep, Keep, Heat, Meat, Beat, Bee, Free, Deep, Seed, Green, Street
Long 'i'	Cried, Pie, Files, Mile, Pile, Bike, Nine, Time, Shine, Line, Slide, Fire
Long 'o'	Boat, Coat, Float, Bone, Cone, Note, Phone, Home, Nose, Rose, Poke, Rope
Long 'u'	Blue, Clue, True, Cute, Cube, Tube, Mute, Flute, Dune, Use, Mule, June

Try to vary the words to include short and long vowels.
(Maybe mix and match with some S.A.T.P.I.N. words too - bonus!)

 ## Now lock in your idea

Scene ideas for my story including Phonics words:

1: ....

2: ....

3: ....

SIMILES

As brave as a big bear	As bright as the sunny sky	As small as a mouse
As soft as a fluffy cloud	As dark as a cave	As soft as a pillow
As tall as a tree	As wiggly as a slinky worm	As messy as muddy boots
As shiny as a bright star	As strong as an elephant	As shiny as a coin
As happy as a puppy with a toy	As light as a floating feather	As sticky as honey
As round as a bouncy ball	As high as a kite in the wind	As bouncy as a ball
As warm as a cosy blanket	As wet as a splashy puddle	As happy as a clown
As quick as a hopping frog	As pretty as a flower	As cold as ice cream
As slow as a snail	As flat as a pancake	As tall as a giraffe
As small as an ant	As loud as a banging drum	As fast as a race car
As sweet as a juicy apple	As slow as a sleepy turtle	As silly as wobbly jelly

Think of your story.
Can you think of any NEW examples where you could use similes?

 Now lock in your idea

Your best ideas for similes for YOUR STORY:

1: ....

2: ....

3: ....

4: ....

5: ....

SYLLABLES

1-Syllable words	2-Syllable words	3-Syllable words
Dog	Apple	Elephant
Cat	Baby	Dinosaur
Ball	Cookie	Butterfly
Car	Mummy	Banana
Book	Daddy	Potato
Mum	Happy	Kangaroo
Dad	Puppy	Animal
Yes	Water	Family
No	Bubble	Ladybug
Eat	Music	Jellybean

🔒 Now lock in your idea

Pick/think of **1-syllable** words for your story:

1: ....

2: ....

3: ....

Pick/think of **2-syllable** words for your story:

1: ....

2: ....

3: ....

Pick/think of **3-syllable** words for your story:

1: ....

2: ....

3: ....

PATTERNED LANGUAGE

- **Sequential actions (Rule of 3):**

  - "First, the bunny **hopped** over the hill. Then, the bunny **skipped** through the flowers. Finally, the bunny **jumped** into a big, soft puddle."

- **Question and answer:**

  - Who is hiding under the bush? It's the hedgehog.
  - Who is hiding behind the tree? It's the squirrel with a nut.

- **Opposites or contrasts:**

  - **Up, up, up** he looked at the sun. **Down, down, down** he slid for fun.

- **Rhyming couplets:**

  "In the forest, dark and **deep**,
  The little fox went fast **asleep**."

- **Counting:**

  - **One by one**, the stars twinkled bright.
  - **Two by two,** the owls took flight.

 # Now lock in your idea

Ideas for patterned language for YOUR STORY: ....
....
....
....
....
....
....

RHYME

Cat, Hat, Mat, Bat	Sheep, Sleep, Deep, Peep	Duck, Truck, Luck, Muck
Hen, Pen, Ten, When	Snake, Cake, Wake, Lake	Bear, Chair, Hair, Share
Dog, Frog, Log, Hog	Ball, Tall, Fall, Wall	Bed, Red, Head, Said
Sun, Fun, Run, Bun	Slip, Dip, Flip, Trip	Pig, Wig, Dig, Big
Tree, Bee, Free, See	Zoom, Broom, Boom, Room	Boat, Float, Goat, Coat
Train, Chain, Rain, Pain	Squish, Fish, Wish, Dish	Fox, Box, Rocks, Socks
Moon, Spoon, Tune, Soon	Fish, Dish, Wish, Swish	Rain, Train, Plane, Chain
Bee, Knee, Flee, Tea	Book, Look, Hook, Cook	Cake, Make, Take, Lake
Car, Star, Far, Jar	Hill, Will, Fill, Still	Ice, Nice, Price, Slice

Think of **YOUR STORY.**

Think of the character, setting etc. and which words rhyme with it. Can you make a 'chorus' at all that you can use within the story?

 **Now lock in your idea**

Scene ideas for my story including rhyming words:

1: ....

2: ....

3: ....

4: ....

5: ....

ALLITERATION

Example 1:

- **Step 1: Pick keywords**
    - Choose important words: Poppy (main character).
- **Step 2: Find similar words**
    - Make a list: "pink," "play," "pigs," "pat."
- **Step 3: Add alliteration**
    - Use similar words: *"Poppy pats the pink pigs."*

Example 2:

- **Step 1: Pick keywords**
    - Choose important words: Timmy (main character).
- **Step 2: Find similar words**
    - Make a list: "tiny," "toes," "tummy," "tap."
- **Step 3: Add alliteration**
    - Use similar words: *"Tiny Timmy taps his tummy."*

 **Now lock in your idea**

Step 1 - Main character name: ....

Step 2 - Find similar words: ....

Step 3 - Add alliteration: ....

ONOMATOPOEIA

Buzz (the sound of a bee)	**Sizzle** (the sound of frying food)
Roar (the sound of a lion)	**Chirp** (the sound of a small bird)
Splash (the sound of water)	**Moo** (the sound of a cow)
Crunch (the sound of biting into something crisp)	**Plop** (the sound of something small falling into water)
Hiss (the sound of a snake)	**Munch** (the sound of chewing soft food)
Boom (the sound of thunder)	**Meow** (the sound of a cat)
Ding-dong (the sound of a doorbell)	**Clap** (the sound of hands hitting together)
Pop (the sound of a balloon bursting)	**Toot** (the sound of a small horn or whistle)
Whizz (the sound of something moving quickly)	**Slurp** (the sound of drinking noisily)
Bang (the sound of something hitting hard)	**Whoosh** (the sound of air moving fast)

🔒 Now lock in your idea

My favourite 5 onomatopoeia words and then used in a sentence:

1: ....

2: ....

3: ....

4: ....

5: ....

Your Story Outline

Go over all ideas (onomatopoeia, alliteration etc.) and see where you can include these for your story.

OUTLINE

Title: ....

Main character name: ....

Villain name: ....

Ally name: ....

Main setting: ....

Beginning of story (what happens) - think of the opposite to the theme eg: if friendship is the theme then the opposite is loneliness, so your character could feel lonely here - what would they be doing?
....
....
....

Inciting Event: ....

Main character needs to (their goal): ....

Because: ....

What happens if they DON'T achieve this goal? ....

Worst case scenario: ....

How/when do they get help with this? ....

OUTLINE

Step 1 to the goal: ....

Obstacle: ....

Consequence: ....

Step 2 to the goal: ....

Obstacle: ....

Consequence: ....

Step 3 to the goal: ....

Obstacle: ....

Consequence (success): ....

The actual ending: ....

The theme is: ....

My plot twist (the 'however'): ....
You decide where the plot twist goes when you write your story).

Scenes I want to include: ....
....
....
....
....

SCENES

Now write your story in **scenes.**

Your Checklist

For each scene think about:

(Hint - You don't have to use every single one in every scene.)

- **Character:** Who is in the scene?

- **Dialogue:** What is your character saying?

- **Senses:** The 5 senses that 'appear' - touch, taste, smell, see, hear.

- **Colours:** What are the main colours?

- **Numbers:** Any numbers?

- **Onomatopoeia:** Boom! crash!

- **The theme:** How can you show the main theme or opposite theme at the beginning?

- **Similes**

- **Alliteration**

- **Syllables:** Keep mainly to 1-2 syllable words (3 ONLY if children would know the word).

- **Shapes:** What are the main/obvious shapes in that scene?

- **Emotions:** What emotion would the character be experiencing?

- **Show not tell:** How can you SHOW the character doing something, NOT just telling?

- **Short and long vowel words:** Cat, cake, etc. Use a variety.

Write Your Story

Follow Your Outline

800 words max.
Go over **all** your notes

Include: Opposite of theme, introduce main character, inciting event etc.

Scene: Start with action - what is you main character doing?

Scene:

Scene:

Scene:

In each scene, if you include **30-33 words,** you would hit the word count perfectly!

Include: Goals, obstacles + consequences etc.

Scene:

Scene:

Scene:

Scene:

In each scene, if you include **30-33 words,** you would hit the word count perfectly!

Include: Goals, obstacles + consequences etc.

Scene:

Scene:

Scene:

Scene:

In each scene, if you include **30-33 words,** you would hit the word count perfectly!

Include: Goals, obstacles + consequences etc.

Scene:

Scene:

Scene:

Scene:

In each scene, if you include 30-33 words, you would hit the word count perfectly!

Include: Goals, obstacles + consequences etc. (plot twist maybe?)

Scene:

Scene:

Scene:

Scene:

In each scene, if you include 30-33 words, you would hit the word count perfectly!

Include: Plot twist? Main theme and ending etc.

Scene:

Scene:

Scene:

Scene Ending:

In each scene, if you include **30-33 words,** you would hit the word count perfectly!

Title: The Lonely Boy and the Little Lost Pirate.

Main character name: Finn.

Villain name: Grumpy Grog the Fisherman.

Ally: Captain Sunny.

Main setting: A small seaside village and a pirate ship.

Beginning of story: Finn feels lonely, sitting by the shore, tossing pebbles into the sea, wishing for a friend.

Inciting Event: A pirate ship crashes near the village, and Finn spots Captain Sunny stuck in the sand.

Main character needs to (their goal): Help Captain Sunny fix his ship and find his lost treasure map.

Because: Captain Sunny promises Finn an adventure and friendship.

What happens if they DON'T achieve this goal? Captain Sunny will be stuck forever, and Finn will stay lonely.

Worst case scenario? Grumpy Grog the fisherman wants to steal the map and traps them.

How/when do they get help with this? A talking parrot flies in with a clue after Step 2.

Step 1 to goal: Finn and Sunny search the beach for ship parts to repair the ship.

Obstacle: The tide washes away the wood.

Consequence: They have to start over, feeling discouraged.

Step 2 to goal: They climb a cliff to find the treasure map. It has blown up there in the wind.

Obstacle: Grumpy Grog traps them with a big net.

Consequence: They get tangled and almost give up.

Step 3 to goal: They get out of the net, helped by the parrot and seek the treasure.

Obstacle: A storm starts, and they have to act quickly to get in and out of the cave before it floods.

Consequence (Success): They find the treasure—a chest of golden coins and wood to repair the ship.

The actual ending: Finn and Captain Sunny share the coins with the village. They all become best of friends.

Theme is: Friendship makes life an adventure.

My plot twist (the 'however'): The talking parrot is Grumpy Grog's pet but decides to help Finn because it likes him better! (This happens after Step 2.)

Scenes I want to include:

- Finn tossing pebbles alone by the sea.
- Captain Sunny's ship crashing with a big "BOOM!"
- The parrot actually helps Finn and Sunny.

Include: Opposite of theme, introduce main character, inciting event etc.

Scene: Start with action - what is you main character doing?

Finn sits by the blue sea. Plop! Pebbles splash. Cold waves tickle his toes. He sighs, "I wish I had some friends to play with." Seagulls squawk overhead.

Scene:

BOOM! A big pirate ship smashes into the yellow sand. Sails flap. Finn smells salty air. "Who's there?" he whispers to himself as he gets closer to the pirate ship.

Scene:

Captain Sunny stumbles out. "Argh!" he groans. His hat wobbles. Finn sees his round, shiny buttons. "Help me, please! I need to repair my ship and find the treasure map!"

Scene:

"I will help fix your ship and look for the treasure map," Finn says. The wood creaks loud. "Wow! Are you sure? Does that make us friends?" Sunny asks. Finn nods with a big smile on his face.

In each scene, if you include 30-33 words, you would hit the word count perfectly!

Include: Goals, obstacles + consequences etc.

Scene:

Finn and Sunny skip together. "Crunch!" go the shells under their feet. They look for some wood to repair the pirate ship. The sun shines bright orange in the sky. "I see some wood we can use - there!" Finn shouts happily.

Scene:

"Whoosh!" Big waves crash in. The wood floats away fast. Finn's feet get wet. "Oh no!" he cries out. "Shall we try again?" Sunny asks. "Yes - Look up there!" Finn says pointing upwards.

Scene:

They climb up high. The rough rocks hurt Finn's hands. "Here is the map!" Sunny says. Finn grabs hold of the map.

Scene:

Grumpy Grog a local fisherman appears from nowhere. "Grrr! Stop there!" His black beard swishing as he shouted. He swings a big square net over Finn and Sunny to trap them. Finn smells stinky fish in the net. Grumpy Grog shouts, "I want that map - give it to me!"

In each scene, if you include 30-33 words, you would hit the word count perfectly!

Include: Goals, obstacles + consequences etc.

Scene:

Finn yells "Help!" Sunny wiggles hard trying to get out of the net. Rocks roll down below the cliff.

Scene:

A red and blue parrot whooshes down fast "That's Grumpy Grog's parrot!" Finn says, feeling scared.
"Squawk!" It pecks the net. Grog shouts, "Stop that!" The parrot helps Finn and Sunny escape. "Wait! Grumpy Grogs parrot is actually helping us!"

Scene:

Sunny pulls free from the net. "Thank you, Mr. Parrot," Sunny says. Sunny then helps Finn.
Grumpy Grog is trapped in the stinky fishing net now. Finn and Sunny grab the treasure map on the ground.

Scene:

Finn shouts, "Yay!" very loud and happy. The map is brown and crinkly. Sunny says, "It's treasure time!" Mr. Parrot flaps its wings with joy.

In each scene, if you include 30-33 words, you would hit the word count perfectly!

Include: Goals, obstacles + consequences etc.

Scene:

"Let's find the treasure!" they all shouted.

Scene:

They all follow the map to a cave. "Shall we go in?" asks Finn. "Yes, but let's all stick together," Mr. Parrot squawks.

Scene:

Just as they all go into the deep dark cave. A storm starts. Heavy rain starts. "We need to search quickly! The water will start rising!" Finn shouted.

Scene:

Mr. Parrot flies ahead to help look for the treasure.

In each scene, if you include 30-33 words, you would hit the word count perfectly!

Include: Goals, obstacles + consequences etc. (plot twist maybe?)

Scene:

"Can you see anything, Mr. Parrot?" Sunny calls out. Finn looks towards the entrance of the cave, water is slowly coming in. "We need to be quick!"

Scene:

Mr. Parrot squawked.

Scene:

"Well done, Mr. Parrot, you found the treasure! And there is lots of wood too! I can repair my broken ship!" Sunny said with glee!

Scene:

Mr. Parrot helped carry tools. Finn helped Sunny repair the pirate ship Sunny arrived on. "Wow! Your ship looks as good as new!" Finn said after the ship was repaired.

In each scene, if you include 30-33 words, you would hit the word count perfectly!

Include: Plot twist? Main theme and ending etc.

Scene:

"We could help others with this treasure. Let's leave it on the beach with a note. I've found my treasure. I've found the most amazing friends in you and Mr. Parrot," Sunny said.

Scene:

"You are my best friends too!" Finn said to Sunny and Mr. Parrot. All of them climbed onboard the pirate ship. Sunny would set sail later that evening.

Scene:

"We will be friends forever," Sunny said to Finn. Mr. Parrot squawked with delight!

Scene Ending:

Finn, Sunny and Mr. Parrot sat on the pirate ship laughing in the bright evening summer sun.

In each scene, if you include **30-33 words,** you would hit the word count perfectly!

FRONT COVER

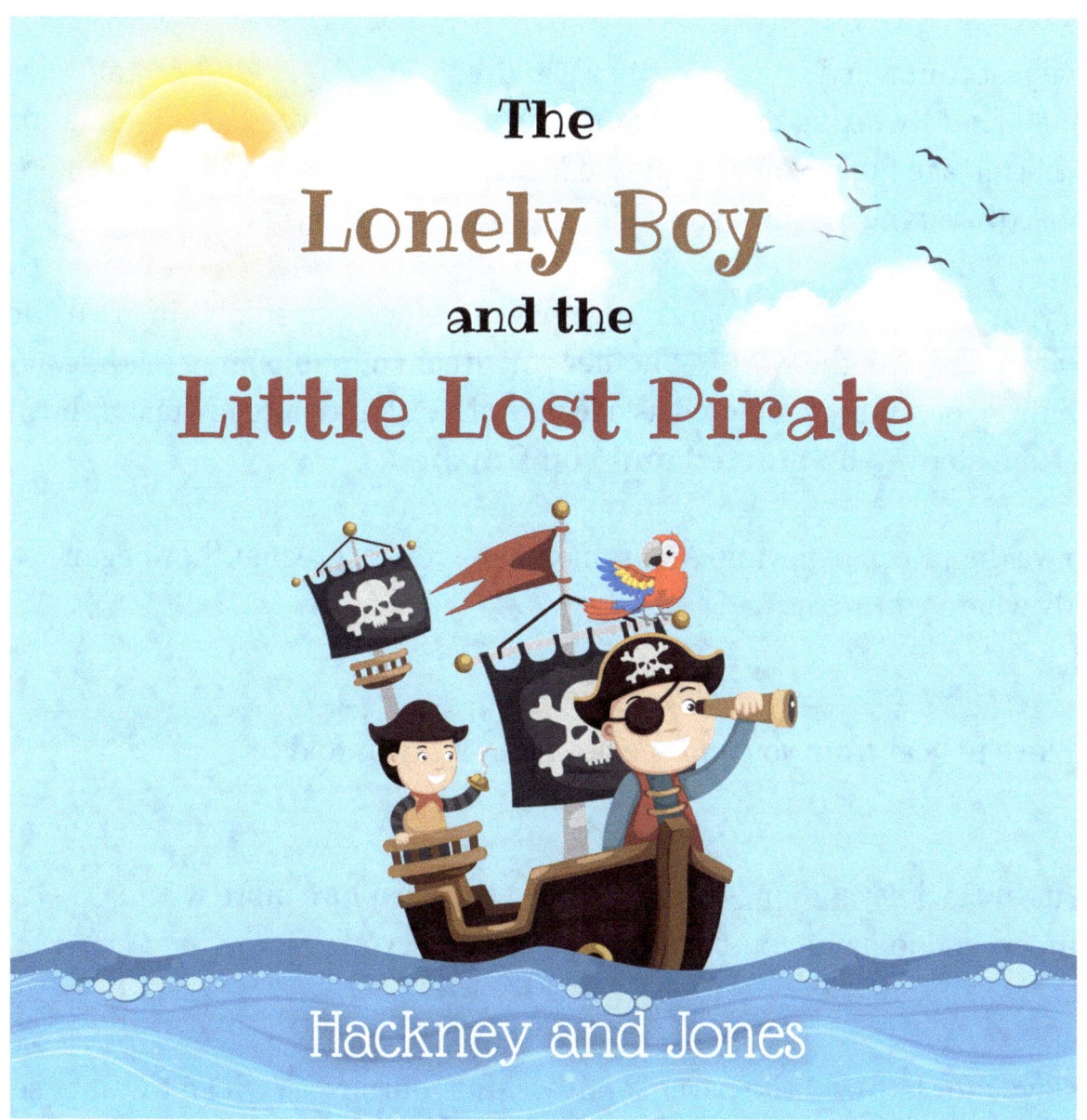

CONCLUSION

Congratulations — You've Done It!

You've just completed How to Write a Children's Story for Adults — and that's no small feat! By taking this creative journey, you've proven that imagination truly has no age limit. You've explored ideas, built worlds, crafted characters, and discovered the magic of storytelling — one page at a time.

Now, your next adventure begins: turning your story into something real and ready to share with the world. Whether you dream of publishing, reading aloud to children, or simply keeping it as a legacy piece, you've already taken the most important step — **you started and you finished.**

Keep writing. Keep believing. And remember — every great author began exactly where you are now.

We'd love to hear from you and see how your story unfolds.

Visit us at Hackneyandjones.com to get in touch, explore more writing resources, and join our community of creative storytellers.

Thank you for letting us be part of your writing journey — we can't wait to see the stories you'll bring to life next.

Claire Hackney & Vicky Jones
Authors | Educators | Publishers
Hackney & Jones

HackneyandJones.com

www.ingramcontent.com/pod-product-compliance
Lightning Source LLC
Chambersburg PA
CBHW051422070526
44584CB00023B/3536